D0615556

HOW TO
WOO
A DUKE

& BE THE TALK OF THE TON

Lady Whistleblower

POP PRESS

Pop Press, an imprint of Ebury Publishing
20 Vauxhall Bridge Road
London SW1V 2SA

Pop Press is part of the Penguin Random House group of
companies whose addresses can be found at
global.penguinrandomhouse.com

Penguin
Random House
UK

First published by Pop Press in 2021

www.penguin.co.uk

A CIP catalogue record for this book is available from the British
Library

ISBN 9781529148596

Printed and bound in Great Britain by Clays Ltd, Elcograf S.p.A.

The authorised representative in the EEA is
Penguin Random House Ireland, Morrison Chambers,
32 Nassau Street, Dublin D02 YH68.

Shall we promenade?

Contents

Tuesday, 8 August 1813

DEAREST READER

Welcome to the definitive guide to navigating the social season. Learn about etiquette in all its forms.

Within these abundant leaves you will be gifted with all the instruction and patronage necessary to take your place in society.

Sort your dandies from your rakes, your merry andrews from your bucks. The menagerie of beau monde is contained within.

So, read on, dearest reader, and swim in the pool of knowledge that will equip oneself **to Woo a Duke** and become the talk of the ton.

Yours sincerely,

Lady Whistleblower

Introduction

Introduction

To "woo" is to seek the favour of a potential suitor, to find a betrothed.

I must first impress upon you that one cannot promenade around ton casting glances at every "tulip" without suitable breeding.

With the guidance in this book we will soon see a visit from cupid, and by cupid I assure you I mean a combination of a heavy-handed mama and an agreeable chaperone.

"He'll do!"

WHAT IS A DUKE AND HOW IS A
DUKE DIFFERENT FROM AN EARL?

There are only *twenty-four* current dukes on this Great Isle of ours and unfortunately most are wedded or ineligible for marriage.

You would do better to focus your energy into bagging one of our *one-hundred-and-ninety-one* current earls. The title 'earl' is the third rank of the peerage. Earls sit smugly in social standing above a viscount or baron, but below duke and marquess.

Are you happy to settle for an earl? Just don't lower your standards to a baron, how dreary!

*"Rest assured, my dear, my bank
balance is as big as my forehead"*

Earl Richingham

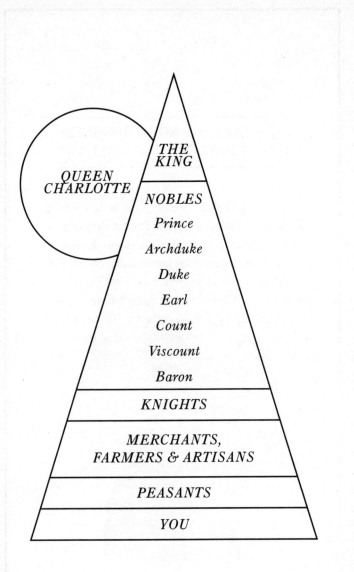

THE
KING

QUEEN
CHARLOTTE

NOBLES

Prince

Archduke

Duke

Earl

Count

Viscount

Baron

KNIGHTS

MERCHANTS,
FARMERS & ARTISANS

PEASANTS

YOU

HOW DOES HER ROYAL HIGHNESS
QUEEN CHARLOTTE FIT IN ALL THIS?

As King George is otherwise deposed with his muddled head, the Prince Regent sits on the throne to make the humdrum decisions. Mostly, these decisions are about dinner and more and more expansive breeches if truth be told. Queen Charlotte, the King's wife, is free to reign over the social calendar and to take her place as the matriarch figure that the ton requires.

*"One is
perpetually
amused"
Queen
Charlotte*

Yass Queen

...Charlotte

HOLD ONE'S CARRIAGES, WHAT IS "THE TON"?

Oh, dear reader, if you are somewhat in the dark about the ton then perhaps wooing a duke is not the right path for you at this juncture? Perhaps a handsome farmhand or clergyman might make one's fan flutter?

To be crystal clear "the ton" originates from the fashionable French phrase "*le bon ton*", or "good manners".

Anyone and everyone pretends to speak French these days, so why not join in? You can boast about being "*le beau monde*" (the beautiful people).

Making Your Debut

PREPARING TO MAKE YOUR
FORMAL DEBUT IN SOCIETY

U ntil now your life will have been coddled, protected and comfortable in your family home, but as you come of age it is now time to be presented at court, find a suitable match and live happily ever after.

Oh, but if it were that simple!

Your debut day is the most important day of all, you will be presented at court to Her Majesty, Queen Charlotte.

The very first presentation to Queen Charlotte was hosted in 1780, whilst she stood beside a ridiculously grandiose birthday cake, which is of course absolutely no laughing matter!

Queen Charlotte's cake
(the people are to scale).

MAKING A FAUX PAS

Catching The Queen's eye is all that matters when presented. Make a faux pas, though and prepare to plummet down in society to unthinkable depths.

Make sure your entrance is notable for its grace and poise and you shall go far.

But beware, make too much of an impression and you can make jealous enemies that would relish in your downfall.

Tittle-tattle and gossip, no matter how false, can destroy your esteemed reputation.

"It's Britney, bitch!"

Lady Britney Spearsmore

THE CORRECT DRESS

To be presented at court one must be elegantly dressed and make a splendid figure. Refinement is key, my dears.

Court attire is very different – wider, plumper and stiffer (and that's just the mamas!) – to modern fashions than, say, a promenade dress. Court dresses must not be worn at other social engagements, and are never worn twice.

As for accoutrements: one's hair MUST be placed up, obviously with a fine selection of your family jewels. Your head is to be adorned with a plume or two otherwise you will be practically naked.

Promenade dress

Court dress

"Do you think they will notice?"

CONCEALING BLEMISHES

Oh, the horror of awakening with a cutaneous eruption the size of a distressed vole on one's face! Fret not, there are beauty regimes to employ in this instance:

1. *Lead and arsenic* – a wonderful way to bleach your face with no side effects.*

2. *Mouche* – a discreet patch of black velvet that one can wear on the face to cover blemishes or damage from lead and smallpox scars. Mouches can be employed to communicate secret messages like, "My face is damaged by lead" or "I have had smallpox".

3. *Fard* – sweet almond oil, mixed with spermaceti (sperm whale head cheese) and honey, applied to the face and left overnight.

Editor's note: there are A LOT of side effects, including death.

*When one's "trunk" is
plenty full of "junk"*

SHOW ME THE MONEY!

When it comes to dowries, normally a young lady will not bring a great deal of money or property to the marriage. (Nor shall the gentleman for that matter. Useless.)

Larger dowries can be either something to seek out or considered suspect; a bribe, perhaps, for selling off unkempt daughters?

A dowry exists to compensate the husband for the upkeep of the wife, and to provide her spending money for the rest of her days.

Pin money is an agreed amount of the dowry that a wife may spend on luxuries without answering to her husband. Such wonderful freedom!

Crying does not indicate that you are weak.

Since birth, it has always been a sign that you are alive

Charlotte Brontë

The Social Season

The Social Season

DECEMBER TO AUGUST

Each and every year, the aristocracy descend upon the ton for a frivolous six-month season of balls, concerts and parties. The social season starts after Parliament have taken their seats in December and runs until midsummer.

The social season has a dual purpose, it is not just to entertain the upper classes and distract them from all the dreariness of owning mansions, but is also an ideal excuse to bring together eligible young men and women with a view to marriage.

"When I say 'bow', one says 'selector'"

A FULL EVENING'S EVENTS

A full evening out in the ton can be a lengthy one, with many events happening in one night.

Dinner will be served at six o'clock and followed by a visit to the opera, a lengthy opera in Italian with no intermission. To wake oneself after all the bellowing, a promenade is oft adopted.

Balls and dances begin at ten o'clock in the evening and can continue till three o'clock in the morning (especially if the band are banging out the classics). The ensemble will play a mixture of waltzes, quadrilles, two-step and UK garage.

The Dowager's Stud Book

Coming out

Not shelved

Engines of War

Didn't come out yesterday

A royal Salute

THE COMING

Four girls to Commoners
The fifth must have a Coronet!

Came out last Season

1870

Apropos de bottes

SEASON

Will conquer or Die.

ROMANCE OR ARRANGEMENT?

The marriage mart is full of bloodthirsty mamas and weary fathers making arrangements for their darling debutantes to achieve the most advantageous pairings. There are dangers abound as dubious poets, dreadful cads and slimy scoundrels may try to catch your eye and even convince oneself that a marriage of love is an option. The current fashion for romance and love in these matters can prove troublesome.

Trust, my dear, a more thoughtful and considered approach with detailed and refined examinations can flush out the chaff and ultimately prove vastly more successful than the foolish flutters of love.

*Overindulgence in social season
can lead to disgrace*

ALMACK'S BALLS

Tickets to the weekly balls at Almack's during the social season are highly coveted, but beware of the patronesses; they run a strict event. Only those deemed to have suitable family connections and behaviour can enter. Those brave enough to attempt the hottest new dance in the ton, the scandalous waltz, will first have to receive permission. Outrage!

BALL CONDUCT

One may expect smooth-running balls as long as one adheres to the customs detailed below:

1. Ladies should never address an unknown gentleman. If she wishes to chat to the rake at the punchbowl, she must first seek an introduction from a chaperone or trusted third party.

2. An unmarried lady of quality will always appear under the protection of a chaperone.

3. Once an introduction is made the gentleman may ask the lady to dance. It is not easy for the lady to refuse this offer, and it may be easier to do the dastardly deed of a dance with a prig than to suffer the embarrassment of a refusal.

FAN FLIRTATIONS

Ladies may communicate secretly with potential suitors through the use of their fan.

Movement	Meaning
Carrying in the right hand in front of the face	Follow me
Carrying in the left hand	Desirous of acquaintance
Twirling it in the left hand	I wish to be rid of you
Drawing across forehead	We are being watched
Carrying in the right hand	You are too willing
Twirling in the right hand	I love another
Drawing across the cheek	I love you
Drawing across the eye	I am sorry
Letting it rest on right cheek	Yes
Letting it rest on left cheek	No
Open and shut	You are cruel
Dropping	We will be friends
Fanning slow	I am married
Fanning fast	It's hot in here

DANCING

If you're not akin to the latest fashion in shuffling one's feet to the music then it is considered acceptable to walk through the dance with elegance, rather than attempt the latest craze and end up looking like a buffoon.

Suffer not, the same dance will not be called twice in the same evening so at the very least you may suffer this indignity only once.

During a dance, if a couple fails to take their place at the start, they have to go to the bottom of the dance.

It is rather bad form to leave the dance before it ends; I am afraid, my dears, that you will have to refrain from calls of nature till the music ceases.

Finally, never be seen without gloves in a ballroom, it simply won't do.

Subtly leaving the ball with a
framed portrait of the duke

MAKING CALLS AND LEAVING CARDS

A lady should start making calls upon arrival in the ton, to notify all and sundry that she has arrived. It is customary to precede your call with a calling card. Give a bad calling card and expect to be turned away like a shameful goose.

Make sure to display your received calling cards from impressive visitors in the entrance hall; you may remark upon them nonchalantly in passing, "Oh, this old thing? Why yes, the duke did pay me a visit. I couldn't possibly tell you more."

Remember to mark the reverse of your calling cards with impressive French phrases like *Felicitation, Affaires, Pamplemousse, Baguette* and *Adieu*.

*"Once this crapulous bottle-ache
clears I shall be sure to call"*

Make sure to make a call to the host the day after the party; so you can check that you acted properly and catch up on the tittle-tattle of those who acted improperly.

Confusingly, morning calls are made in the afternoon (to allow one's hangover to subside).

Intimate calls are made later in the afternoon and should last half an hour – just long enough to spill the tea. If you are mid-flow and another caller arrives during your visit it is polite to make your excuses and leave.

GENTLEMEN CALLERS

The day after a ball you may expect to see gentlemen callers at your door, who are keen to access your heart and weigh up your prospects as a potential match. A gentleman should always precede his visit with a calling card.

However keen you are, a lady should never visit a gentleman's house. Be patient, my dears!

Ahead of their call, a gentlemen can send a gift, but should never send an expensive gift as it may be considered by those with looser lips than mine to be a bribe on the lady's affections. The gentlemen should stick to books, flowers, sweets and anything else available in the forecourt of a horse and carriage refuelling station.

*"I hereby invite one to
take down my particulars"*

"*Shall we go the bumpy way home for some 'hand on elbow' action?*"

TOUCHING GENTLEMEN
IN THE ALLEY

Gentlemen should never touch a single lady. Even if the pair are courting, there should be no touching! The only time this is passable is during a promenade; if the road is somewhat uneven, the gentleman may offer his arm… it's surprising how many uneven roads there are in the ton, highly surprising indeed.

Gentlemen should offer to carry any bags or luggage the lady may be carrying. It is also deemed polite for a gentleman to offer his arm to help a lady down from a train, carriage or some particularly tricky steps.

*"It's been eighty-four
years since my debut"*

*Lady Sonia Spinster
23 years old*

SPINSTERSHIP

Enduring over three seasons without an engagement for marriage is enough to prepare the lady in question for spinstership.

Spinstership is best spent with a wealth of cats and the study of new sewing techniques. You may also look forward to being a chaperone to your sister's children and casting judgement upon them.

The story for single gentlemen is a different one as they remain eligible, and become more so the more wealth they accumulate. A wealthy old curmudgeon with a dodgy ticker is an eligible thing indeed.

FEARING "THE CUT"

During the social season you will meet and greet many fine souls, but there will be some who you simply cannot abide, and then you have to make the choice to either make a cut or to continue with your charade.

The ultimate snub is to give someone the cut. This is where one person looks directly at another and does not acknowledge the other's bow. It is such a breach of civility that only an unforgivable misdemeanour can warrant the rebuke.

Not without the gravest cause may a lady cut a gentleman. But there are no circumstances under which a gentleman may cut any woman who, even by courtesy, can be called a lady.

MISTAKING DAYDREAMING
FOR "THE CUT"

It's important for one not to confuse absent-mindedness with an intentional cut.

Preoccupied persons are oft able to pass others without being able to regard them. There are others with forgetful memories, or daydreamers, who may pass even those to whom they were much attracted.

A real cut is very different to a forgetting of oneself. It is an insult to its intended victim. A cut is crystal clear. A cut is a direct, blank look and a refusal to acknowledge the other party.

Happily, a cut is practically absent from polite society, and if you intend on staying in society I suggest you steer clear of such things.

"THE CUT" IN FOUR PARTS

If you are supremely certain that a "cut" is of the utmost importance, there are four main ways to action one:

1. *The direct cut* – stare your acquaintance in the face and simply pretend they are a stranger to you.

2. *The indirect cut* – when presented with the offending party, look away and pretend you have not seen them.

3. *The sublime cut* – gaze upon a beautiful cloud and remark upon the heavens till the person being "cut" has passed.

3. *The infernal cut* – find an excuse to look away from your incompatible suitor at the opportune moment and begin to adjust a boot or bow.

"I will CUT you"

Baroness Blunt

Does it really matter what these affectionate people do?

So long as they don't do it in the streets and frighten the horses!

Mrs. Patrick Campbell

Courtship

Courtship

IT ALL STARTS AT THE BALLS

Once an introduction to an eligible gentleman has taken place at a ball or some such similar event, the couple may begin to spend some time with one another.

If a couple dance together more than twice in an evening and refuse to dance with others then the couple are considered "courting". Alternatively, it may be viewed that the lady is somewhat "unchaste" but that is the subject for another, filthier, more thrilling book.

Courting oft takes place over a short period, but if the couple are spending hours in each other's company they will be considered engaged (with or without the formal offer being made).

TRUST ONE'S CHAPERONE

Your chaperone is there to help you avoid ruin and keep you pure (even if in appearance only) and, also, to direct you towards a successful pairing.

At a ball, one must remain by their chaperone's side till one begins to dance. It's permissible to walk around and receive refreshments with your previous dance partner, particularly if he has caught your affections.

When the next dance commences one must be returned to one's chaperone's side. At this point you may compare notes on your potential match and decide if a second dance is advised.

Trust your chaperone's advice as they are at an advantage, being cold of heart, and may easily spot a rake or a beastly buck!

THE IMPORTANCE OF SWOONING

When tight of corset and light of head, a swoon may be conjured at any occasion or time that one requires.

By swooning at the opportune moment one may demonstrate a gentile and innate pureness of spirit. If a swoon is carried out correctly a certain amount of attention can be directed one's way by parties of interest. Falling uncontrollably into the arms of a handsome buck in any other circumstance would be scandal indeed, but what are you to do? One is at the mercy of one's feminine frame…

Now fetch me the vapours!

"Oh mercy, I appear to have swooned
onto your doorstep... at three o'clock"

Lady Brazen Bootycall

SUSSING YOUR SUITOR

When wooing your potential suitor there are some golden rules to remember:

1. Find a match with a reasonable similarity of disposition and means to oneself. What chance does a match have if both parties are not reading from the same page?

2. Beware the overly friendly types. Platonic relationships do not make for good marriages. Hearts must be at least slightly engaged.

3. Stay within your levels of intelligence. A partner with an all-consuming intellect will be both a bore and a condescending crutch. Ditch the professor.

4. Steer clear of poets. All talk and no breeches. These sorts are prone to flights of fancy and oft vow to jump on swords for you but never seem able to do so.

5. Try not to actually fall in love. It will cloud your judgement and lead to a faulty match.

6. If you are in love, don't indulge in over-sentimentality or, God forbid, tell your suitor how you truly feel. Nothing will chase them away faster.

7. Overlook your beau's minor faults. They may be guilty of little sallies of peevishness or ill humour, but these things can be ironed out with time and patience.

8. Major faults are a forewarning! A man of vicious character will remain a man of vicious character. No matter how much time you spend improving such a beast, they will not make a good and exemplary husband.

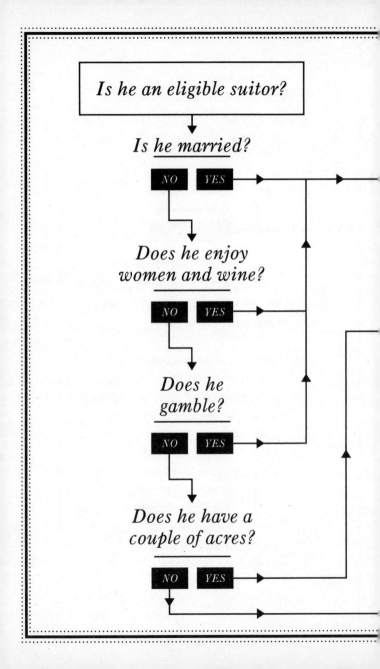

Is he an eligible suitor?

Is he married?

NO   YES

Does he enjoy women and wine?

NO   YES

Does he gamble?

NO   YES

Does he have a couple of acres?

NO   YES

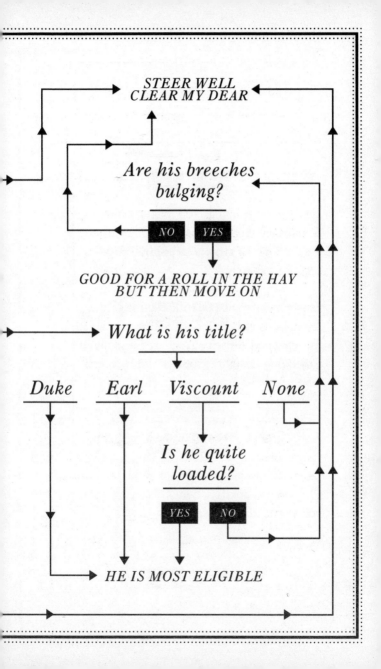

THE ENGAGEMENT

If a gentleman takes too long to offer marriage there will be mutterings around the ton that the chap is some sort of rotten sort or jackanape.

Engagements must be forthcoming or the reputations of both parties may be damaged, for what sort carries on a courtship without a wedding in sight? Floozies and fops, that's who.

As a courtship progresses past the fruity letters and bountiful gifts of flowers, a gentleman should make an appointment with the girl's father to formally ask for her hand in marriage, for whom is possibly better placed to decide her destiny than her father?

"Congratulations, your father says
we are getting married"

THE WEDDING

Once engaged, the happy couple should expect to be wed within three weeks. Any longer and it will be seen as dilly-dallying.

All invitees should receive a written letter, personally inviting them to the ceremony. Keep the guest list small, not just to save on paper, but because a showy, large guest list is simply uncouth.

If your engagement is an "irregular" one or, let's say, you're in a rush to be married within nine months, then you might consider eloping to Gretna Green, where the marriage laws are slightly more relaxed and banns (alerting all in the ton to your hasty matrimony) need not be read.

Preparing to show one's ankles
for the first time

71

Courtship is to marriage...

as a very witty prologue to a very dull play

William Congreve

Marriage

HAPPILY EVER AFTER

After the wedding, the marriage may commence.

Marriage marks the transition of a girl beginning her new life as a lady, even more so as one is to become the lady of the house. She is to be responsible for managing the servants, the household itself, and the health and general well-being of all in the house, whilst also fending off the new husband's advances into the folly of creating an heir!

There is not a sight more uncouth than that of a man and his wife struggling for power. For pure matrimonial harmony ensure your marriage is founded on companionship first over lusty, filthy desires. Filth.

"Watcha doing?"

RULES FOR WIVES

Some essential rules for wives to adhere to, which will ensure a happy and long marriage:

1. A dinner will require a lady to dress appropriately. To appear in one's underskirts is simply unacceptable.

2. After dinner, wives will retire to the drawing-room, leaving their men to their port and manliness.

3. Ladies will **NOT** refer to any of the sordid matters they may have overheard whilst the men drink their port.

4. A wife should be blind to her husband's affairs. How else is a marriage expected to last?

5. A married woman may take a lover **AFTER** she has produced an heir.

Stuck with a bore

*"So yeah, methinks the Arsenal need a good
strong back-line and an attacking wing if
they are to be ahead this fine season"*

CARNAL NASTINESS

B race yourselves, dears, for advice on intimate engagement lies ahead. If you are experienced in such matters it will do you well to claim innocence within the marital bed. A balance must be struck between being crushingly shy and a brazen hussy.

For the best preparation, before the night, ask your maid for advice and to explain what goes where and for how long. For one must not be ill-equipped.

A modern idea is that a wife has ownership of her body and therefore the final say in what goes on with it, so make sure you are ready to consummate; don't be in too great haste to "tug the furry fruit from the forbidden tree".

Dear readers, that is enough euphemism and analogy for one page. Let us move on and spare more blushes.

Pushing the button to
"arrive at Euston station"

Rules for Gentlemen

Rules for Gentlemen

ENGLISHMEN AND MANNERS

A gentleman is a well-educated man of good family, whose income is from property. God forbid that he toils for a living. Being a gentleman also requires decorum, culture, courtesy and that the fellow abide many rules.

General manners:

1. Losing your temper is a sign of poor upbringing. Gentlemen are discreet and polite.

2. Never stand in front of a roaring fireplace with your back to it. Especially if you are toasting nuts.

3. Never refuse a gift as it only causes more embarrassment.

4. A gentleman never boasts. Your talents may be discussed by others.

"I'm the very, most humble man there is!"

5. Do not pick at your teeth, nose or buttocks. Mercy me!

6. Personal hygiene is a must. Hair should be combed, teeth brushed and nails clipped.

7. A gentleman's outfit should be immaculate, but not so fashionable that it is remarked upon.

8. When promenading, gloves are essential but a cane is optional.

At dinner:

1. When seated at a dinner table, discreetly place your napkin across your lap.
Do not flap it around, one is not a bird.

2. Never spit food out in plain sight of your company. Find a pot plant or quiet corner to dispose of the offending item.

3. Always drink as quietly as possible. Leave the slurping to horses and dogs.

4. Introductions to ladies should always be accompanied by a bow, never an extended hand.

5. When a lady takes her leave of a room, rise from your seat to show your respect.

6. When conversing with ladies, keep it simple! Discuss the food and weather, never politics or science.

"Sir, one's plums are simply divine"

TYPES OF GENTLEMEN

There are many types of gentlemen to be found roaming the ton. Here is a brief guide to some of the tribes on offer. Beware, there are nuances ahead:

Dandy
A Dandy is a man of fashion, but also a man of charm and wit. Spotted at ten paces by neckwear with absurd knots and flourishes.

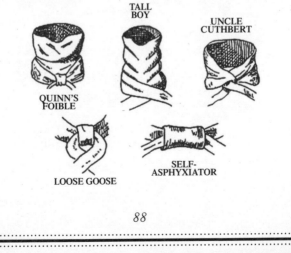

QUINN'S FOIBLE

TALL BOY

UNCLE CUTHBERT

LOOSE GOOSE

SELF-ASPHYXIATOR

Tulip

A pink that has rather gone off the boil.
Fashionable but also taking to last season's
fashions.

Rake

A man with few morals, likely to be found in
a gambling den, heavy with mead and loud of
song. He is wont to spend his inheritance on
women and wine whilst incurring lavish debts
in the process.

Buck

A man who pursues pleasure, debauchery,
fighting and blood sports. A buck, like a rake,
may be pleasing to some but not to all.

FURRY POCKET

HALF-COCKED

QUALITY STREET

FARMER GILES

BASSETT RIM

DEWESBURY QUIFF

FEATHERINGTON FRUMP

VANILLA GUY

HEAD-WEAR

No gentleman should be seen in public without his hat. A gentleman wears a beaver hat if he is to be taken seriously about the ton.

A gentleman's hat gives us an essential insight into his personality, interests and background before he even utters a word. Highly useful when we are sifting through the crowds for a suitor.

Beware, an over-sized tall hat does not necessarily reflect a gentleman's "biological assets", in fact, perhaps he is overly compensating for something? Simply look for a pleasing, fashionable, modest topper and the man underneath is sure to be a keeper.

To be truly elegant one should not be noticed

Beau Brummell

If people turn to look at you... it is because you are too fashionable!"

Remarkably, also Beau Brummell

Scandal!

PURITY AT ALL COSTS

No virtuous young lady should be alone with an eligible gentleman. More important than being pure is being seen to be pure.

A lady's reputation is a tender thing indeed, and a more ruthless gossipmonger than I can be viciously cruel to a debutante caught *in flagrante delicto*.

Most scandals, hereafter in the following pages, come from the grimy details of adulterous carryings-on and acrimonious divorces. I am sure that you, as a pure being, will not want to read on so as to keep your chasteness intact.

Still here? Then let's drop the breeches and raise the petticoats of scandal…

"*I hear that the pair were sharing
her muff in the park. The shame!*"

DIRTY OLD EARL GROSVENOR

All the details of a sordid affair undertaken by the Duke of Cumberland and the wife of Earl Grosvenor, the richest man in the ton, have come to light. Much to the delight of society, who can now dine out on all the devious details.

During the divorce proceedings, Lady Camilla D'Onhoff told the court she "saw Lady Grosvenor lying upon her back on a couch in the drawing-room, with her petticoats up, and the Duke of Cumberland's breeches unbuttoned, his body was in the motion of carnal copulation." Quick, pass the vapours!

As retaliation to this revelation the Duke of Cumberland revealed Earl Grosvenor's penchant for the odd "piece of muslin" and his famous chat-up line, "How do you do, my little wicked? Will you go and drink a glass of wine with me?" Dirty old Grosvenor.

*"I'll take a duke over
an earl any day"*

Henrietta Grosvenor

PARMESAN POEMS

The Marquess of Blandford got himself in a spot of bother when he became entangled with a married woman, Lady Mary Anne Sturt, the wife of a sitting MP. He foolishly vowed to give up his inheritance if she agreed to elope with him.

As a final embarrassment to the Marquess, the finer details of his anguished and tortured love letters to Lady Mary have been made public, including the method of delivery: they were hidden away in gifts of Parmesan cheese. To those that have read them, this isn't the cheesiest thing about his appalling prose.

*"Oh, I can smell that
you've read my letter, my dear!"*

"Oh blast and bother.
It's all true!"

PUBLISH AND BE DAMNED

Harriette Wilson is a popular mistress to many of the nobility at the top of the ton.

After several of her lovers withdrew financial support, she threatened to publish her eye-opening memoirs in more and more lavish instalments.

She has blackmailed each "member" prior to publication and is demanding payment to remove their dalliances from the upcoming book.

One such "member" is General Arthur Wellesley (if rumours are true, soon to be the Duke of Wellington, no less), who was not about to play such a game. He called her bluff and returned the blackmail letter with "Publish and be damned!" scrawled upon it.

It is to published soon and I simply can't wait to be appalled by his behaviour.

BEAU BRUMMELL'S FOLLY

The gentlemen of the ton were clambering to watch the original dandy, Mister Beau Brummell, dress himself. Folly indeed. It is alleged that he requires over five hours to dress and he washes his boots in champagne. What a dreadful waste.

Beau's downfall occurred at a masquerade ball. Beau was quaffing with his selected curated set of friends (including Lord Alvanley). The Prince Regent approached the group and performed a "cut" on Beau, and so in response, Beau turned to Lord Alvanley, and quipped, "Alvanley, who's your fat friend?"

With that petty insult, Beau was cast from society for the rest of his days. It pays to watch your mouth!

"One is slaying one's game"

Beau Brummell,
overheard in Regent's Park

Reputation is as brittle as it is beautiful

Jane Austen

One false step involves her in endless ruin

Jane Austen

Duels

Duels

RESTORING ONE'S HONOUR

Duelling is the civilised way to settle matters of honour.

Duels are not fought to kill the opponent but merely to achieve satisfaction and restore one's honour from the perceived besmirchment.

Duels are, of course, illegal, but there are certain rules to observe:

1. Duels are fought using either swords or pistols.

2. To challenge your opponent, throw your glove down in front of them or slap them around the face with it.

3. You must choose an acquaintance to be your "second". The job of a second is to decide the place and time of the duel and decide if the weapons are suitable.

"That's for eyeing up my Darren"

Lady Sharon from Essexham

TO THE DEATH?

The offended party can choose what conclusion the duel can be fought to:

1. To first blood. The duel is fought till one party is wounded, even if only slightly.

2. Until one party is so wounded that they can no longer continue. More than merely a flesh wound.

3. To the death. A mortal wounding.

In the case of pistol duels, each party would fire one shot. During a pistol duel to have more than three shots is considered barbaric, and, if you both require more than three shots, simply ridiculous and a day at the shooting range may be fruitful.

*"I fear we have misunderstood the
rules of duelling dear Paul"*

*Lord Barry and Lord Paul Chucklington,
during their duel to the death with putters.*

Sir, I would challenge you to a battle of wits

But I see you are completely unarmed

Lord Sassington of Sassy Hall

Glossary
of Terms

Glossary of Terms

Accomplishments
A young lady is expected to have many
diverse talents such as playing the pianoforte,
watercolours, sewing or admiring kittens.

Accoutrement
An accessory to an outfit: parasols,
feathers, jewels and so on.

Barouche
A regency convertible. A carriage with a
folding hood. If one wishes to be an absolute
baller.

Betsy
A detachable lace collar made up of lace
ruffles to be worn with a dress.

Bit o' muslin / piece of muslin
A lady who pleases gentlemen for monetary
payment.

Bourdaloue
A travelling female chamberpot.

Breeches
Short, tight trousers that display all the right bulges in the right areas. Oh mercy me!

Courses
Monthly courses. Simply put, my dear, periods.

Cabriolet
A gentleman's two-wheeled carriage. The sports edition with one horsepower and a blacked-out canopy.

Capped
Putting on one's best hat to "catch" a husband.

Chaperone
A respectable elder who escorts an unmarried young lady.

Chit
An impertinent or unruly young girl.

Coming out
A lady's first entry into society.

Cups
To be inebriated. To be laden with wine.

Dandy
A gentleman who apparently cares more
about his appearance than most other things
on earth.

The dark walk
Finding oneself in the wrong side of town.
A walk that if seen could be a possible
reputation-breaker.

Diamond of the first water
The finest debutante of the season.

Dowager
The wealthy widow. Keen on exclamations of
shock and unnecessary fuss.

Facer
A good old-fashioned punch to the face.
Expertly delivered right on the nose.

Fashionable hour
Between four o'clock and seven o'clock it is
the done thing to be seen promenading or riding
around the ton.

False calves
Getting more junk in a gentleman's lower
leg trunk.

Fop
See "dandy".

Harridan
An unreputed, grumpy old woman.

Inexpressibles
Ladies, well, you know, undergarments.

Jackanapes
A gadabout, a scamp.

Leading strings
Leading strings are straps used to aid children
learning to walk.

Missish
To be prim or prudish.

Modiste
The magician who makes one's dresses.

Monocle
A single eyeglass worn specifically to be plopped into drinks when unexpected things happen. I say!

Muff
Somewhere to keep one's hands warm.

Promenade
To walk in public – to promenade with a significant other is a wonderful way to announce your intentions to the ton.

Quadrille
A square dance, for many couples.

Rake
A good-time Charlie, a gentleman who enjoys social events. Usually with a flourish of broken hearts in his wake.

Snuff
Powdered tobacco, stuck up one's nose.

Swoon
Fainting, but done in style. Merely for effect.

The ton
The ton refers to the British high society. It is derived from the French term "*le bon ton*" or "good manners". One can be a member of the ton, go to ton events, or even have good ton.

With child
The ton's way to describe pregnancy without having to utter such vulgar words. I apologise.

If a book is
well written

I always find it too short

Jane Austen

About the Author

Lady Whistleblower, Countess of Whistleblower, is an English socialite and scandal merchant. Nothing happens in the ton without Lady Whistleblower knowing about it. Famously, a muse of Lord Byron and the subject of over *fourteen* sonnets.

Acknowledgements

One would like to thank all of the debauched and depraved members of the ton, for without whom I would not be able to continue to publish my writing:

For who can forget when Lady Halliwell removed herself from the singing troupe, *The Spice Dames*, the awful fuss and unmentionable scandal that the Duchess Melanie Bee caused. It kept me in the column inches for months, my dears!

The Bishop of Bognor, whom when it came to affixing a new tapestry to his wall, fell backwards, cassocks aflutter, onto his drawing-room desk. A desk adorned with many varieties and sizes of potato. Sadly, one of the larger King Edwards found their way into the Bishop's interior. Such a disaster, and one to be thought of solemnly in our nightly prayers.